NOTTINGHAM FROM THE AIR

First published in Great Britain in 2008 by
The Breedon Books Publishing Company Limited
Breedon House, 3 The Parker Centre,
Derby, DE21 4SZ.

Acknowledgements

The authors would like to express their sincere thanks for the help they have received in the production of this
book. Particular gratitude is due to Richard Napper - 'simply the best aerial photography pilot around', Chris Jagger,
Marie Lewis, Karen and Suzanne – plus Jenny Bracegirdle who took the magnificent photograph on Page 132.
A big thank you also, to all at Breedon Books for their patience and wisdom, as well as the citizens of Nottingham
who help to make the city such a fantastic place to live and visit.

ISBN 978-1-85983-668-2

Printed and bound by Scotprint, Haddington, Scotland.

NOTTINGHAM FROM THE AIR

Photographs by
Ian Bracegirdle

Text by
Dave Bracegirdle

breedon **books**
PUBLISHING

Contents

The city of Nottingham is known and respected throughout the world for so many different reasons – for young and old alike. Movie-goers and historians have been enthralled by the legend of Robin Hood – still one of the main tourist attractions in the area – while the splendid learning facilities available ensure there is always a healthy queue of talented youngsters wishing to move to Nottingham to further their educational dreams, resulting in a vibrant nightlife and social culture. Retail, business and sporting achievements have also helped put on the map a city which is now home to a multi-cultural society – almost 300,000 strong.

Nottingham from the Air looks at many of the city's landmark buildings and sights – as well as giving a flavour of what life is like for the people who live there.

Above: The magnificent front entrance of the Theatre Royal.

Left: The new Victoria Halls student accommodation.

Like so many great cities, Nottingham boasts an extraordinary contrast of both ancient and modern buildings.

It been at the forefront of some of the most innovatively designed modern architecture.

Aerial photography highlights the designer's creativity to maximise the limited space available in the city centre and surrounding area.

The Inland Revenue Headquarters

The Inland Revenue building was built on a previously derelict area and opened in 1995, providing accommodation space for up to 2,000 staff.

The project has created its own urban quarter with pedestrianised streets, and is located between the canal and the stunning backdrop of the castle.

It includes four 'L' shaped buildings, two larger blocks with their own central courtyards, and an amenities building housing restaurant, bar, crèche and sporting facilities.

At the corner of each of the office blocks there are circular towers, which not only contain spiral staircases to all floors but also act as an important aid to the ventilation system by helping to pre-cool the structure and circulate fresh air into the complex.

The amenities building is manufactured from a light tensile fabric, suspended from four steel masts.

The Council House

The Nottingham Council House was opened in 1929 by HRH the Prince of Wales (later King Edward VIII and the Duke of Windsor). Its 200ft dome dominates the city-centre skyline.

Designed by Thomas Cecil Howitt and built in the neo-baroque style, the Council House was erected on the former site known as The Shambles – Nottingham's meat market.

The ground floor is made up predominantly of a shopping mall, named the Exchange Arcade, while the upper floors contain council chambers and offices, dining rooms, tea rooms and a stunning ballroom where the grandest of visitors, including royalty, heads of state and stars of stage and screen, have been entertained.

Old Market Square

The Council House sits proudly at the eastern end of the Old Market Square – known locally as 'Slab Square'. Covering an area of over 22,000sq metres, it is said to be the largest in the country and was extensively renovated in 2007.

A popular meeting place for tourists and locals alike, the Old Market Square has played host to a wide variety of functions, celebrations and festivities down the years. Between February and April 2008 it was host to 'The Nottingham Eye', a 60-metre high wheel offering panoramic views of the city. Many thousands enjoyed a 'flight' and return visits of the Eye have been planned.

Victoria Halls

With so many students coming to Nottingham to further their education, top-class accommodation is essential and the Victoria Halls buildings offer excellent facilities in three tower blocks adjacent to St Ann's Well Road.

Are the students aware that the mischievous designers have shaped the top of the accommodation to look like irons?

Crowne Plaza

The Crowne Plaza on Wollaton Street is one of a number of new city-centre hotels to have risen in recent years. This 210-bedroom building is also renowned as one of the East Midlands' premier conference and meeting venues.

Strathdon Hotel

Handily situated on Derby Road, close to the city centre, is the Strathdon Hotel, with its unique figure-of-eight design. Built on the site of the old Albany Hotel, it opened in 1969.

ng²

The ng² business site has been recognised as an outstanding piece of modern architecture. Located on Enterprise Way, just off Queens Drive to the south west of the city centre, there has been rapid development with many household companies relocating there. Among them are Mercedes Benz, whose stylish, almost-circular showroom is pictured.

Trent Bridge

Completed in 1871, Trent Bridge is the principal river crossing for all traffic entering the city from the east. Built of iron and stone, it is actually in West Bridgford not Nottingham, and it carries the A60.

Both of the city's professional football teams, plus the county cricket venue which shares the same name as the bridge, lie within close proximity.

Lady Bay Bridge

The Lady Bay Bridge used to be known as the Trent Bridge viaduct and was a railway connection linking Nottingham with Melton Mowbray. For around a decade it was unused, until the wrought-iron bridge was converted for road traffic use in the late 1970s and renamed Lady Bay Bridge.

Wilford Suspension Bridge

Linking Welbeck Road with the Victoria Embankment, the Wilford Suspension Bridge was opened in 1906 enabling water to be brought across the river from Wilford Hill Reservoir.

Old newspaper reports tell of organised swimming contests between the bridge and Trent Bridge, a few hundred yards upstream. The currents of today would certainly prohibit such foolhardiness!

Regularly used by pedestrians and cyclists the bridge has deteriorated quite badly in recent times, and in July 2008 it was closed on safety grounds, with Severn Trent Water agreeing to make it structurally sound before reopening it.

Above: Magistrates' Court

The new Magistrates Court on Wilford Street has also been part of the regeneration programme alongside the banks of the canal. It was built between 1993 and 1996 on redeveloped land close to the canal. It contains 16 adult courtrooms, plus six family and youth courts.

The white-roofed building to the right of the photograph is the Coroner's Office.

Left: Riverside Developments

The area surrounding Canal Street in the southern part of the city centre has undergone a remarkable transformation in recent years. British Waterways, the canal authority, joined up with the city council to replace derelict and disused buildings with a new wave of luxury apartments, bars, bistros, clubs and office space.

The sign on the old British Waterways warehouse remains, although little else remains in this trendy part of town to indicate how important a part the canal played in Nottingham's distant past.

Trinity Square

During 2008 the major city centre development was centred around the Trinity Square area, where brand new shopping, car parking and leisure facilities – plus even more student accommodation – were being constructed. As these photographs show, the available space is limited, yet the finished product is expected to become the largest major retail development in the city for 30 years.

Nottingham used to be synonymous with several of the country's most established and well-known companies. Nowadays the likes of Raleigh, John Player and Sons, Boots the Chemist and Home Ales no longer operate from within the city centre.

Raleigh manufactured bicycles in the city from 1886 until 2003, when the factory on Triumph Road was demolished to make way for the University of Nottingham's expansion of Jubilee Campus.

John Player and Sons

The tobacco manufacturers John Player and Sons were once one of the major employers in Nottingham. Nowadays the company is part of the Imperial Tobacco Group and has moved out of the city centre.

However, these bonded tobacco warehouses (right) remains on Triumph Road, close to the Jubilee Campus.

Biocity

Boots the Chemist were formed in Nottingham in 1849 by John Boot and then transformed into a global brand by his son, Jesse.

Nowadays the parent company is known as Alliance Boots plc and there are no longer any significant operations within the city.

Some former Boots researchers and university spin-off companies have spawned a thriving pharmaceutical, science and biotechnology sector called BioCity, which is based on Pennyfoot Street close to the city centre.

Above: Alongside the Colwick Loop Road stands an oil refinery, maintained by Total UK.

Right: Also on the Loop Road, a sewage farm.

Previous Page: Home Ales
The Home Brewery was founded in 1875 and this head office building was built on their Daybrook site on Mansfield Road in the 1930s. In 1986 the owners sold the company to Scottish and Newcastle Breweries. Gradually production moved to other factories around the UK until closure a decade later. Nowadays the premises are used by the Nottinghamshire County Council.

County Hall

County Hall is situated just across the road from Trent Bridge Cricket Ground in West Bridgford and is one of the East Midlands' most popular venues for corporate conferences and training courses. Still a Notts County Council building, it contains reception facilities and administrative offices.

The foundation stone was laid in 1939 but delays, initially due to the war and then because of funding issues, meant that completion was postponed until 1963. Copper was used in the construction of the roof, which, due to weathering, has subsequently turned green over the years.

Alongside County Hall stands another administrative building – the CLASP Building. (CLASP being the acronym for Consortium of Local Authority Special Projects).

Theatre Royal

Originally built at a cost of £15,000 and opened in 1865, the Theatre Royal was the brainchild of two Nottingham lace dressers, William and John Lambert. It was one of the most stylish and luxurious theatres of its day and subsequent generations have visited the venue to see leading artists perform in touring productions, musicals, pantomimes and operas.

The classic façade and corinthian columns still exist today, although the building itself has undergone many facelifts over the decades.

At the back of the theatre is the Royal Concert Hall, opened in 1982. It was built on the site of the old Empire Theatre of Varieties, a music hall venue which ran for 60 years until its closure in 1958.

The Cornerhouse

Opposite the Concert Hall stands the
Cornerhouse, an entertainment complex that
houses a 14-screen cinema, nightclub, bars,
restaurants, beauty salons, shops and a casino.

Above: The Showcase Cinema
There are several cinema complexes within the city centre but one of the most popular is the Showcase, situated on a retail park beside the A52 at Lenton.

Right and overleaf: Trent FM Arena
Since the opening of the National Ice Centre in 2000, Nottingham has also had a world-class concert venue, which has already played host to many of the world's top headlining artists. The 10,000-capacity arena now bears the name of a local radio station which entered into a four-year sponsorship deal in 2008.

Over 40,000 full-time students attend Nottingham's two Universities, the University of Nottingham and the Nottingham Trent University, formerly known as Trent Polytechnic

The University of Nottingham

The University of Nottingham is the fifth largest in the United Kingdom and is made up of the Jubilee Campus and the University Park Campus, which are a couple of miles to the west of the city centre.

King's Meadow Campus, which is much smaller, and the Sutton Bonington Campus, 12 miles away, complete the Nottingham components of the university, although it also operates from two overseas campuses – one in China and the other in Malaysia.

Jubilee Campus

The Jubilee Campus was built on a former brownfield site, having previously been owned by Raleigh Industries for the manufacture of bicycles. Her Majesty the Queen opened this campus on 9 December 1999.

The teaching blocks are known as The Exchange and are adjacent to The Djanogly Learning Resource Centre, which is the circular building jutting out into the lake (right). This contains an extensive library.

Spanning Triumph Road is the Gateway Building (below), shown during construction. The completed project was opened in September 2008.

Previous Page: The University's Jubilee Campus continues to expand with major developments continuing as the photograph demonstrates.

Right and far right: Among the feature buildings on the Jubilee Campus are The Djanogly Learning Resource Centre and the National College for School Leadership.

Specialist courses undertaken on the Jubilee Campus are Computer Science and Information Technology as well as Business Studies.

Overleaf: Identification of the halls of residence is made easier from the air as they have clearly been built in the shape of the numbers 3 and 8. Southwell Hall is the 3 and Newark Hall the 8.

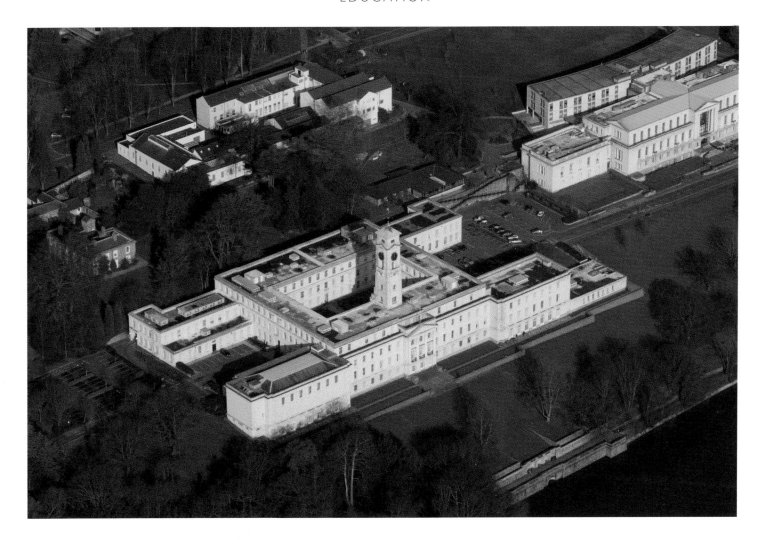

The University Park Campus

Approximately 500 metres from the Jubilee Campus is the University Park Campus. These aerial shots show the two white feature buildings on the campus. To the left is the Trent Building, while the Portland Building is on the right.

The Trent Building was the original home of University College Nottingham when it first moved to the University Park site in 1928. It still remains a key landmark building and plays a vital role in the expansion of all arts subjects.

The Portland Building houses the Students Union and the International Students Bureau as well as shops, banks, bars and restaurants.

Part of the University Park Campus, the Lakeside Arts Centre, featuring the award-winning D.H. Lawrence Pavilion, has a picturesque location and contains a 250-seat theatre, exhibition gallery and amphitheatre.

Queen's Medical Centre

Queen's Medical Centre lies to the west of the city centre alongside the busy A52. The first purpose-built teaching hospital in the UK, it brings together patient care, teaching and research all under one roof. It welcomed its first patient in August 1978 and now, together with Nottingham City Hospital NHS Trust, provides hospital services to over 600,000 people and specialist services to over two million people. Queen's has over 1,300 beds and employs nearly 6,000 people.

Either side of the A52 at Clifton Boulevard you can see the Queen's Medical Centre to the right and the university's science and engineering faculties on the left.

The university's teaching hospital, the University of Nottingham Medical School, is part of the Queen's Medical Hospital.

Nottingham Trent University

The majority of the Nottingham Trent University buildings are located close to the heart of the city (locals would direct you to pop just behind the Theatre Royal and Royal Concert Hall). A further campus can be found just across the city at Clifton, while the Brackenhurst Campus is home to the School of Animal, Rural and Environmental Sciences and is around 10 miles away at Southwell. Two of the feature buildings on the city campus are currently undergoing extensive renovations.

Above: The Newton building became a dominant presence on the city skyline when it was built in the 1950s. Gradually it has become dwarfed by some of the surrounding structures but it remains an important landmark and is being redeveloped to include state-of-the art learning and teaching facilities, plus lecture theatres and IT resources.

Right: The Arkwright building was built between 1877 and 1881 and has been used by the University College Nottingham and the Nottingham and District Technical College. In 1941 the building was partially destroyed during the Blitz, with 45 people losing their lives there.

Like the Newton building, this is also a Grade II listed building, and the restoration of it will be painstakingly slow to ensure all the conservation requirements are met.

Above: Nottingham Science Park
Opened in June 2008 by HRH The Duke of Kent, the Nottingham Science Park is located at Highfields – between the City of Nottingham Tennis Centre and East Drive – and contains the Toyota Academy. Intended to provide specialist vocational training for college students aged 14–16 years old, in partnership with local schools, and as a National Training Academy for Toyota, the facility will be used by up to 600 students and apprentices each year.

Left: Rosslyn Park
Perhaps the most startling of the myriad of schools and colleges in and around Nottingham is the Rosslyn Park Primary and Nursery School at Aspley.

Nottingham Castle

High on a hill, to the south east of the city centre, is the 11th-century Nottingham Castle. Visitors flock to this popular tourist attraction which became synonymous with Robin Hood, a hero of English folklore.

It was here that Robin pitted his wits against the Sheriff of Nottingham in his bid to win the hand of the fair Maid Marian, and a statue of Robin is situated just outside the perimeter wall.

Inside the grounds you can see the victorian bandstand and the remaining buildings, including the mediaeval gatehouse, guard room and dungeons. The cannon positions still remain, as does the Miller's Cottage.

Above: Ye Olde Trip to Jerusalem

Visitors to the castle invariably stop for refreshment at one of the world's oldest and most famous hostelries, Ye Olde Trip to Jerusalem. Carved into the rock and connected to many of the sandstone caves at the foot of the castle, the inn has the date 1189AD painted on its exterior walls. This date bears relevance to how the 'Trip' got its name, for it was the year of the ascension to the throne of King Richard I, known as Richard the Lionheart, and one of his first acts as King was to crusade against the Saracens who at that time occupied the Holy Land of christian religion.

Nottingham Castle was a stronghold favoured by the King and legend has it that the brave knights and men at arms who rallied to his call to fight in this Third Crusade gathered at the castle to rest and 'have one for the road' before embarking on their 'trip to Jerusalem'.

Left: Nottingham Castle viewed from the west. The Victorian bandstand can be seen at the top of the photograph.

Wollaton Hall

Wollaton Hall lies about two and a half miles to the west of the city centre and is set in over 500 acres of parkland. Built between 1580 and 1588 for Sir Francis Willoughby, it is home to both the city's Natural History Museum and the Industrial Museum. It is a Grade I listed building.

Camellia House

The Camellia House is located close to Wollaton hall. Built in 1823, this is the oldest cast-iron glasshouse in Europe. Its internal columns are hollow, allowing the rainwater to gather in tanks and provide water for the camellias. Vandals damaged the building in 2001, smashing most of the glass panes, and the fully renovated Camelia House could not be reopened until 2008.

Arboretum

Just a short walk from the city centre lies the 'Arboretum', a beautiful park which was opened in 1852. Within the grounds are an aviary, a bandstand, a Chinese bell-tower and some spectacular flower beds.

Green's Windmill

In Sneinton, a suburb to the east of the city, stands a restored and working 19th-century tower windmill.

Originally built and owned by the Green family, it became derelict until purchased by Nottingham City Council in 1979. It was renovated and reopened to the public and is now part of a science centre.

Memorial Gardens

In 1920 the Clifton Estate offered a piece of land for sale on the Nottingham side of the Trent and it was bought by Jesse Boot (son of the founder of the Boots company). He presented it to the City of Nottingham to be preserved forever as an open space for the benefit of the citizens of Nottingham.

A memorial was built, honouring those from the city who had fallen in the 1914–18 conflict initially, but later the names of those who had died in both the 1939–45 war and the Korean conflict were added. The memorial stands 46ft high and is 58ft wide. On the second Sunday of November each year, the City and County of Nottingham's Federation of Ex-Serviceman's Association hold a Remembrance Service at the Memorial garden gates. Within the gardens stands a statue of Queen Victoria (seen at the very bottom of the photograph) – this had stood in the Old Market Square for 48 years until it was relocated in 1953.

War Rooms

Nottingham's War Rooms were built during the 1950s on two levels, one below ground and one above, with the main control room spanning both. Built on Chalfont Drive, the concrete rectangular blocks were designed to protect the occupants from a blast and from the consequent nuclear fall-out. Had the sirens ever sounded, local government officials would have headed for this building – and safety! Nowadays most of the building is empty and unused, although it has been preserved as a reminder of the Cold War days.

Colwick Hall

Once the ancestral home of Lord Byron, Colwick Hall sits in over 60 acres of parkland, just a couple of miles from the city centre. Built in the latter part of the 18th century, it was privately owned until sold to the Nottingham Racecourse Company in 1896. The hall became a public house and the rest of the buildings were used to accommodate the grooms and jockeys.

Today the property is owned by the Pearl Group and is in constant demand for corporate functions, weddings and private events.

Religion

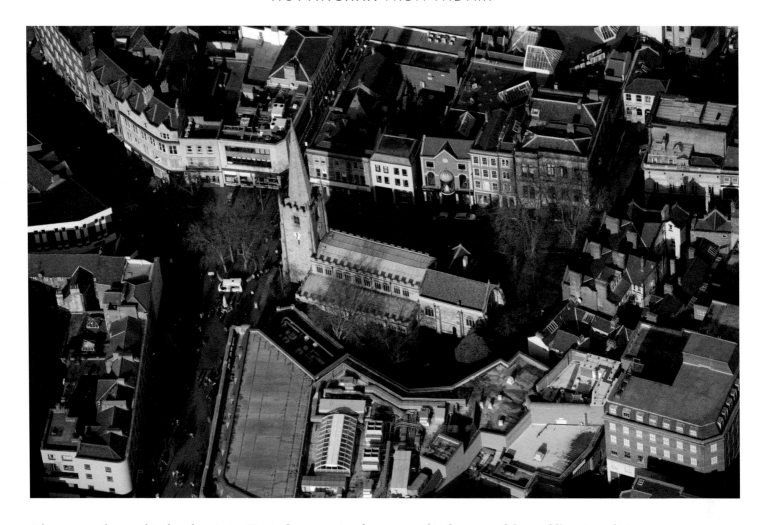

Like most modern multicultural societies, Nottingham contains places to worship for many of the world's major religions.

Above: St Peter's
St Peter's Church, in St Peter's Square, claims to be the oldest continually occupied building in the Nottingham area, having been rebuilt shortly after 1175 when the original church on the site was burnt down. Situated just outside the Broadmarsh shopping centre, St Peter's is passed by thousands of pedestrians every day.

Previous Page: St Mary's
The Parish Church of St Mary the Virgin, on High Pavement in the Lace Market, is the oldest foundation (dating from the eighth or ninth century) but the present building is believed to be the third on the site, although it is still more than 500 years old.

It is considered to be the mother church of the city and civic services are held there, including the annual welcome to the Lord Mayor of Nottingham.

St Barnabas
St Barnabas's Roman Catholic Cathedral, off Derby Road, was built between 1841 and 1844 at a cost of just £15,000.
It is located on the corner of Derby Road and North Circus Street. The cathedral is a Grade II listed building.

Above: St Andrews
St Andrews Church stands on the junction of Mansfield Road and Mapperley Road and was built in 1871.

Right: Nottingham Islamic Centre
The Nottingham Islamic Centre is based at the Noorani Mosque on Curzon Street, off St Ann's Well Road. Its distinctive green dome is said to be similar in design to the Mosque of the Prophet Muhammed in Medina, Saudi Arabia.

A day's shopping in Nottingham would not be complete without a visit to either of the city's two major shopping centres.

The Victoria Centre

The Victoria Centre was built between 1967 and 1972 on the site of the former Nottingham Victoria Railway Station. It comprises 116 shops and encompasses an area of 981,000sq ft. The clocktower (left) is the sole remaining feature of the old station, although the Hilton Hotel remains close by.

Above the shopping area stands a row of 25-storey flats, which rise to a height of 250ft above the shops.

The Broadmarsh Centre

The Broadmarsh Centre, which can be seen in the centre-left of this picture, was also opened in 1972 and is located just to the south of the Market Square. It was developed on derelict land that historically was of a boggy consistency, hence the name.

During construction many forgotten caves and cellars were rediscovered and they have been preserved into one of the city's main tourist attractions, the City of Caves, which actually runs underneath the shopping centre.

Although much smaller than the Victoria Centre (88 stores, 484,000sq ft), pictured centre-right opposite the Broadmarsh, plans have been submitted to totally redevelop the area and transform the Broadmarsh into a new £700 million complex, dwarfing its predecessor. In the coming years, the current site is to be redeveloped into one new super-complex with a street-like form and more than 400 shops over three floors.

Bridlesmith Gate

Popular with the fashion-conscious, Bridlesmith Gate is a busy pedestrian street in the heart of the city. Pictured to the lower right of the photograph, it is home to many of the current trend of designer shops and is sometimes referred to as 'Posh Man's Alley'. The original Paul Smith shop opened here.

Lace Market

The development of the waterside area and the old lace market has made this a trendy part of the city for dining, drinking and socialising – as well as to make the most of the opulent boutiques and fashion houses that have brought their wares to sell.

Above: Street Market
Small traders will always find a way though – such as these stall holders on one of many small street markets that still exist.

Right and previous page: Sainsbury's
More and more out-of-town supermarkets are being built outside the city centre – such as this one at Daybrook.

Sports aficionados delight in the facilities on offer in Nottingham. The city boasts two historically famous football teams, a Test Match cricketing venue of the highest order, the country's premier Ice Stadium, plus the national water sports centre, a leading racecourse and greyhound stadium, an international tennis centre and excellent opportunities for hockey, rugby and athletics enthusiasts, among others, to fulfil their sporting dreams.

Football
The city's two Football League clubs have their homes just 300 yards apart on opposite banks of the River Trent.

Meadow Lane

Meadow Lane has been home to Notts County since 1910. The ground was badly bombed during World War Two and left in an unplayable condition, and it has also fallen foul of flooding at various times over the years. Ground redevelopment in the 1990s culminated in the demolition of the old Main Stand, which was replaced by The Derek Pavis Stand housing conference and banqueting facilities, as well as the dressing room area, media facilities and main reception.

Since 2006 Nottingham Rugby Club have also played their home fixtures at Meadow Lane, following the closure of their old home at Beeston.

The City Ground

Despite being just outside the city limits, Forest's ground is called the City Ground and was first used by the club in September 1898. Although there was the euphoria of an FA Cup win in 1959, the Reds enjoyed the most successful period in their history under the management of Brian Clough during the 1970s and 1980s when they were twice crowned Champions of Europe.

The Executive Stand was built in 1980 at a cost of £2 million – largely funded by those on-field successes. The stand was renamed The Brian Clough Stand in the mid-1990s as a lasting tribute to the man whose talents had made it possible.

The ground was given a major facelift in readiness for the 1996 European Championships as it staged three matches in that tournament, featuring Turkey, Portugal and Croatia.

With a capacity of just over 30,000, many spectators feel that the ground is just too small to support ambitions of returning to the big time. Prospective new sites have been considered to build a new stadium for the club, with the favourite seemingly at Clifton, close to the A453 on the western outskirts of the city.

Left and above: Cricket - Trent Bridge

Trent Bridge cricket ground is the home of Nottinghamshire County Cricket Club and is a regular venue for Test and One Day Internationals.

It was first used as a cricket ground in 1838. William Clarke, captain of the All England Team, had married Mary Chapman, proprietor of The Trent Bridge Inn, and developed the meadow at the rear of the hostelry as a suitable playing field.

Both Nottingham Forest and Notts County also used the venue for their home fixtures at various times during the 19th century – and in 1897 it even hosted an international match when England defeated Ireland 6–0. In 1899 the ground staged its first Test match, with England and Australia playing out a draw.

The ground has been subjected to many facelifts in recent years. The Fox Road Stand was opened in 2002. The most recent developments have included the building of a brand new stand on the Bridgford Road side of the ground which was opened by Prince Phillip in June 2008, plus the installation of six permanent floodlight towers, which will keep Trent Bridge at the forefront for the 21st-century passion for day/night cricket.

Overleaf: Radcliffe Road Stand

Opened in 1998 by former Notts great Sir Garfield Sobers, the Radcliffe Road Stand was built at a cost of £7.2 million. The stand houses the indoor Trent Bridge Cricket Centre, as well as media facilities and a reception area, plus it is an excellent location from which to view the cricket.

The National Water Sports Centre

The National Water Sports Centre is based at Holme Pierrepont. The main centre and Regatta Lake were opened in 1972, although the official opening ceremony took place a year later.

The venue hosted the World Rowing Championships in both 1975 and 1986, by which time the White Water Course had also opened.

Set in 270 acres of parkland, there are three separate pieces of water; a 2,000-metre regatta sailing facility, a 700-metre white water canoe slalom course, plus a water ski lagoon equipped with a slalom course and ski jump.

The National Ice Stadium

The home city of Olympic gold medallists Jayne Torvill and Christopher Dean, Nottingham has become the ice capital of the UK. The building also houses the Trent FM Arena, formerly known as the Nottingham Arena. This 10,000-seater facility is not only used by the world's biggest stars as a leading concert arena, but it has also staged many major sporting events including boxing promotions, WWE events, Masters football, Harlem Globetrotters Shows, plus athletics and darts tournaments.

Aside from the skating facility, leading Ice Hockey side, the Nottingham Panthers, are based at the stadium.

The City of Nottingham Tennis Centre

The City of Nottingham Tennis Centre can be found on University Boulevard, to the south west of the city centre.

In the run-up to Wimbledon the leading players on the men's tennis circuit have pencilled Nottingham into their diaries for many years.

Previous winners include Pete Sampras, Goran Ivanisevic, Greg Rusedski and the Croatian Ivo Karlovic who won in both 2007 and 2008, although the LTA's plans for the immediate future have sadly resulted in the tournament being dropped from their calendar.

Greyhound Stadium
Above: Set alongside the racecourse, dog-lovers can experience the thrills of live greyhound racing three evenings per week all year long.

Horse Racing
Overleaf: The horse racing fraternity gather at Colwick Park, just a couple of miles to the east of the city centre. The racecourse sits in the 280-acre grounds of Colwick Country Park and backs onto the National Water Sports Centre at Holme Pierrepont.

   The racecourse opened in 1892. Both national hunt and flat race meetings are held, with regular meetings usually accommodated between March and November.

Above: The Park Tennis Club
The Park Tennis Club is situated in the valley of Nottingham's Park Estate, close to the castle, and has around 200 members making full use of the eight all-weather courts.

Right: Nottingham Forest Academy
Nottingham Forest's youngsters learn their trade at the academy, off Wilford Lane. In the top right of the photograph is West Park, a much-used and popular cricket venue in West Bridgford.

Suburban

Nottingham's population draws ever closer to the 300,000 mark and increasingly more people are being located in high-rise city centre accommodation, as well as a vast array of student apartments.

The suburbs contain many traditional housing estates, both private and council-owned.

Aerial photography illustrates the clever way in which the builders have made maximum use of the available space.

Flats and Apartments

Far Left: Marco Island
The Marco Island apartments run along Huntingdon Street onto Lower Parliament Street and is located next to the Royal Mail depot.

Left: These high-rise flats were built in the mid-1960s and are located in Radford, between Hartley Road and Norton Street. Locally they are referred to as 'The Four B's'.

Above: In sharp contrast to the houses surrounding it, this block of flats dominates the skyline between Sneinton and Thorneywood.

Right: Another new development nearing completion is this tower block off Gregory Boulevard.

The Victoria Flats were built above the Victoria Shopping Centre and run the entire length of the building from north to south. They rise to a height of around 250ft and dominate the city skyline.

These luxury south-facing riverside apartments are shown during the final stages of their completion in 2008. The complex will be known as River Crescent and is located at Trent Park, Colwick, close to the racecourse.

Housing Estates

Above: These houses are in Colwick, stretching from Colwick Lodge to Belvoir Lodge.

Right and far right: Similar shots of this semi-circular estate – the front part of which is Sneinton Dale.

Older properties in The Park, pictured above. The developers of these city properties obviously were not under quite as much pressure to cram as many houses as possible into the space available.

Whereas these newer residents, pictured right, just to the west of the city centre at Farndon Green, do not have to look quite so far for their nearest neighbour.

Left and above: There are 'roundabout' five houses in the centre of Collin Green at Woodthorpe.

Overleaf: A panoramic shot of the city taken from the east. On the horizon you can see smoke billowing from the Ratcliffe on Soar Power Station.

Above and left: These developments in Aspley and Bulwell are located on the outskirts of the city and are typical of the way in which a limited amount of space has been used to full effect.

Overleaf: HMP Nottingham

HMP Nottingham is located at Perry Road in Sherwood. It opened in 1890 as a city gaol but was reconstructed in 1912 and until 1997 served as a closed training establishment for adult males. In 1997 it re-rolled as a category B local prison and now serves the courts of Nottinghamshire and Derbyshire.

Transport

Parking

Like all major conurbations, Nottingham faces a continual challenge to find sufficient road and parking space for the ever-increasing quantity of vehicles that frequent the city's streets.

With parking space at a premium, more and more multi-storey facilities are essential, like these at St James' Street (**above**), Upper Parliament Street (**right**) and Trinity Square (**far right**).

Roads

Nottingham is served by the M1, with junctions 24, 25 and 26 providing access into the city centre.

Far Left: The A52 is the major dual carriageway which runs through the city. Here it forms an interchange with the A6514 Clifton Boulevard.

Left: The picturesque Western Boulevard to the west of the city centre.

Trams

Trams have once again become fashionable as an alternative form of public transport and a means of minimising private vehicle use in the city centre.

Operated by Nottingham Express Transit, the city's fleet of 15 trams are managed from the depot on Wilkinson Street. It was built on decontaminated land, formerly disused industrial land between the former Shipstone's Brewery and Cusson's soap factory.

Canal

There has been a canal flowing through Nottingham since 1796, providing a means to transport coal and building materials around the region.

In times of heavy rainfall the canal would rise and cause parts of the city to flood so eventually parts were filled in and built over.

Nowadays a narrow stretch remains, called the Nottingham and Beeston Canal, which links with the River Trent and is largely used by recreational craft only, several of which can be seen moored in the marina, adjacent to Castle Bridge Road (**far left**).

Above: River Trent
One of England's major rivers, the Trent cuts a swathe through the city of Nottingham as it winds its way from its source in Staffordshire until it joins the River Ouse to form the Humber Estuary.

Right: Bus station
Nottingham City Transport and Trent Barton are the principal bus operators within the city boundaries and they operate out of both the Broadmarsh Shopping Centre and the Victoria Centre where, here, you can see buses lined up at the busy stop at the rear of the building.